Soldiers and Uniforms:

South Carolina Military Affairs,

1670-1775

CAPTAIN FITZHUGH McMASTER, U. S. Navy, Ret., lives in Columbia, South Carolina.

Soldiers and Uniforms:
South Carolina Military Affairs, 1670-1775

Fitzhugh McMaster

TRICENTENNIAL BOOKLET NUMBER **10**

Published for the South Carolina Tricentennial Commission
by the University of South Carolina Press
Columbia, South Carolina

Contents

Chapter I

The Militia
Under the Proprietors

The English colony established in South Carolina in April 1670 was located on territory claimed by Spain and surrounded on the landward side by numerous Indians, some of which were reputed to be maneaters. The small group of approximately 140 English and Barbadians quickly fortified the roughly triangular site of 9 acres, located on the west bank of the Ashley River, with earthworks and palisades, and the 12 cannon furnished by the king were mounted in the embrasures.

The Proprietors furnished 200 firelock muskets (flintlocks), 58 swords, 200 spearheads (the 7-foot wooden shafts would have to be made by the colonists), 200 collars of bandoliers (these each carried 12 premeasured charges of powder and shot, dangling across the chest, and were known somewhat sacrilegiously as "The Twelve Apostles"), and twelve suits of armor (probably breast and back plates and morions). In addition, every able-bodied man was to be armed with a good firelock having a bore equivalent to twelve shot to the pound and ten pounds of powder and 20 pounds of shot. Locke's Fundamental Constitutions of 1669 specified that "all male inhabitants and freemen of Carolina, above 17 years of age and under 60, shall be bound to bear arms and serve as soldiers whenever the grand council shall find it necessary."

Although no description of the militia organization of this period is extant, it is probable that there were four main

groups, or companies, one for each of three sides of the
defensive area with the fourth in reserve under the command of the governor. There were undoubtedly additional
small groups who acted as pickets, or scouting parties outside of the fortifications, who could cover the outlying
houses until an attack in force was made. Other than the
possibility of some of the former army officers wearing
their old uniforms, the militia wore the clothing of the
period with a bandolier over one shoulder. They were
armed with firelock muskets and swords or hatchets. Inside
the fortifications, the pikes were also available and the
company officers probably wore the breast and back plates
and morions at this early date.

In August 1670, a Spanish expedition from St. Augustine
arrived to stamp out the new colony. Apparently impressed
by the fortifications and the militant attitude of the colonists and their friendly Indians, the Spaniards remained
outside the bar until driven off by a storm. Their Indian
allies departed shortly thereafter when the iron cannon in
the fortifications were "scaled" (fired with reduced powder
charges to blow the rust out of the barrels).

Governor Joseph West in March 1671 reported that he had
"reduced the people into two companies that they may be
better disciplined. We cannot yet make in the colony 150
men that are fit to bear arms. . . ." Later that same year, a
short war was fought with the Kussoe Indians, with commissions being made out for two captains to command the
companies of volunteers that were sent on the expeditions.
Following the return of the troops, the council ordered all
persons not a member of the council to appear in arms in
their several companies at the times and places appointed
by their commanding officers for better informing them in
the use of arms and other exercises of military discipline;
all smiths were to attend and "fit" the muskets. The
campaign had also shown that bandoliers were both incon-
venient and unsafe for keeping ammunition and they were

to be replaced with cartouche boxes containing twelve paper cartridges.

Five rendezvous points were established in June 1672 where the colonists of outlying lands were to gather in case of an alarm; two were at distant plantations on the west bank of the Ashley River, and the other three at Charles Town (Albemarle Point), New Town (James Island), and Oyster Point (the site of present-day Charleston). Shortly thereafter, the militia was reorganized into six companies and the Governor's Life Guards. Commissions were made out for a lieutenant colonel, a major and five captains; the lieutenants were to be appointed by their commanding officers and the names of the men in the companies were to "be so listed as may be most helpful for them speedily to repair to their colours upon any alarums."

The number of militia companies was reduced to three in April 1675. This reduction was apparently an administrative change for better discipline as the population of the colony was increasing.

In December 1679, Proprietors ordered that the site of Charles Town be changed from Albemarle Point to Oyster Point as a defensive measure. The seat of government, together with most of the ordnance, was accordingly changed in 1680. By 1682, the population had increased to an estimated 1,000 to 1,200 people; using a ratio of 1 to 5, a militia strength of 200 to 250 men seems probable. The first recorded militia act was passed in 1682, but no details are known. This is also true of the militia acts of 1685, 1687, 1690, and 1691, all of which were temporary acts, generally effective for two or three years but which could be extended by reviving or continuing the acts.

An act was passed in November 1685 which recognized the Spaniards as a probable enemy and authorized three lookout stations to be built and garrisoned on the coast between Sullivan's Island and Port Royal. The colonel, lieutenant colonel, or major of each regiment, or regiments, in

that part of the province was to order the officers of each
company in turn to furnish a sergeant and four privates for
each lookout station to so serve for two weeks; each man was
to be armed with a musket, a sword or hatchet and a cartouche box with twelve charges of powder and shot. This act
supplies some details of the lost militia act of 1685, to which
it frequently refers. At this date, there were two small regiments, with the line between Berkeley and Colleton counties
as the line of demarcation, and the Governor's Life Guards.
The population in 1685 has been estimated at 2,500, with
roughly 500 men in the militia.

During a period of almost anarchy in 1689–90 when the
governor and factions of the colonial parliament and population were at odds and many of the temporary laws had
lapsed, the governor proclaimed martial law in February
1690 and "the same did cause to be published at the head
of every company of the militia." No blood was shed but
civil affairs did not settle down until the beginning of 1695.

The militia act of 1696 called for all inhabitants of the
colony, aged 16 to 60, to be enrolled in the militia company
of the district in which they resided, and to be armed with
a good sufficient gun, lock cover, and cartouche box at least
16 cartridges of good powder and ball, a belt, four spare
flints, and a sword, bayonet, or hatchet. Companies were to
muster and drill every two months and regiments at least
once a year.

The militia was estimated to have numbered 1,500 men in
1698 but may have been reduced somewhat in the ensuing
three years by smallpox, a disastrous fire in Charles Town,
yellow fever, and hurricanes which resulted in between 350
and 500 deaths in the colony. However, John Lawson, who
visited the city in 1700, later wrote: "They have a well
disciplined militia; their Horse are mostly gentlemen, and
well mounted, and the best in America, and may well
equalize any in other parts. Their officers, both infantry and
cavalry, generally appear in scarlet mountings, and as rich
as in most regiments belonging to the crown." ["Mountings"

refers to the clothing issued to soldiers; therefore, militia officers were wearing scarlet uniforms in 1700. A portrait of Colonel William Rhett, painted during the early eighteenth century and now owned by the Carolina Art Association, shows him wearing a steel breastplate over a scarlet coat.]

The militia act of 1703 was similar to the act of 1696 but more detailed. Larger cartouche boxes, holding 20 cartridges, were required, and all officers of the regiments of foot, except ensigns (who carried the flags), were to carry a half pike (spontoon) and be attended by a boy, not exceeding 16 years of age, who carried the arms and accoutrements proscribed for all members of the militia. The commander-in-chief was empowered to station not more than 20 men as lookouts along the coast between the Santee and Savannah Rivers at such times as he felt it necessary.

The patrol act of 1704 called for ten men from every militia company, each provided with a good horse, a pair of pistols, a carbine, a sword and a cartouche box with at least twelve cartridges, to patrol their company's district in case of an invasion or to prevent a slave uprising; however, trusted slaves could be armed and used to reinforce the militia.

In August 1706, a combined French and Spanish force attacked the colony. Three separate landings were bloodily repulsed and the enemy fleet fled when seven small ships, their crews reinforced with militia, sailed to attack them. Contemporary accounts give an incomplete picture of the militia organization at this time. There were two regiments of foot, the northward (Craven and Berkeley counties) and the southward (Colleton and Granville counties) as well as one independent company in the Huguenot settlements on the Santee River. The northward regiment was composed of two companies in Charles Town and at least seven in the country. There is mention of only one company from the southward regiment being present during the attack.

A militia act passed in 1707 was essentially the same as

the act of 1703 except that the provisions for lookout stations were the subject of a separate act. Eight lookout stations were established between the mouth of the Port Royal River and Bulls Island, and six worn out cannon were mounted near houses on that same section of the coast to sound the alarm in case an invasion fleet was sighted.

The strength of the militia in 1708 was reported to be about 950 men; viz., two regiments of foot consisting of a total of 16 companies averaging 50 men each, nine patrols of ten men each, and the French Protestant independent company on the Santee consisting of 45 men and a patrol of ten men. There was some difficulty in finding enough good men willing to accept captain's commissions in the militia —a problem which existed from time to time until the Revolution, inasmuch as the responsibilities were great and the rewards, other than honorary, were small. A motion was made in the Commons House to pay for the drum, flag, and halbards (a combination spear and axe, mounted on a 7-foot pole, carried by sergeants of infantry) of each militia company but it was voted down. Unfortunately, no description of these company flags exists.

A near civil war occurred in 1710 over the question of which one of two men was governor. The alarm guns were fired, the militia was called out, and the drawbridges to the city were raised preventing entry from the countryside. A comic opera situation resulted with the followers of the non-governor marching around the outside of the walls trying to get in, while the supporters of the governor followed them around on the inside to prevent them from entering. The stalemate was broken when dissidents on the inside lowered the drawbridges and let in those on the outside. The two companies of town militia were drawn up with muskets loaded and flags flying, and as the "invaders" streamed past them, somebody tore one of the flags from its staff. A few of the muskets were fired without command, but no one was hit. The captain, by threatening with his sword, recovered the flag. The invaders proceeded to Granville Bastion with threats of seizing it but desisted when a show of force was made. What might have turned into a bloody affair ended with only a few minor cuts and bruises.

During the Yamasee War, the militia numbered between 1,200 and 1,500 white men and, in theory, could have been doubled by enrolling and arming an equal number of trusted Negro slaves. Some Negroes were taken into the militia and in 1715 two companies of about 30 Negroes each, with white officers, were included in the expedition which peacefully persuaded the Cherokees to withdraw from the war and turn against the Creeks. One of these Negro companies remained in the Cherokee nation as part of the force left there and half of the other Negro company was left in the garrison of Fort Moore (on the Savannah River) when the main forces returned to the settlements in the spring of 1716.

In March 1716 legislation was enacted calling for a force of 100 men, volunteers if possible (otherwise to be drafted) from the two regiments of militia, to be sent to relieve the 80 men in the Cherokee nation and to assist the Cherokees when they attacked the Creeks. Five forts, including Fort Moore, were to be erected on the frontiers by nine officers and 117 men from the militia (volunteers if possible, otherwise to be drafted), who were to garrison them until November 1716.

The militia act of 1716 was quite similar to the act of 1707 as to age, arms, and accoutrements except that only twelve cartridges were required in the cartouche box and a powder horn with a quarter pound of powder and a shot pouch with bullets proportional were added. All regimental officers of foot (ensigns excepted) were to be armed with a fusil and other necessary accoutrements instead of the half pike previously carried. These changes were undoubtedly the result of experience gained in the Yamasee War.

An act of August 4, 1716, authorized the payment of £1,000 sterling for 32 rebel Highland Scots (indentured for seven years) purchased by the governor to serve as soldiers in the defense of the province. Any who distinguished themselves by their valor, bravery, and obedience were to have

their term of servitude reduced to four years. It was estimated in the latter part of 1716 that the effective strength
of the militia did not exceed 1,400 men.

In December 1716 an act authorized the appointment of
Rangers to guard the frontiers. Rangers were volunteers or
men drafted from the militia to serve a specified number
of months. They received extra pay for providing their own
horses and ranged or patrolled between two camps on the
frontier. The first mention of them in South Carolina occurs
in the Commons House Journal in November 1716 and in
this case they were to serve for one year. Two captains, two
lieutenants, and 100 men were authorized but fewer were
actually raised.

Men were drafted in 1717 as replacements for the garrisons of the forts and for the Rangers. An additional two
officers and 48 men were to furnish themselves at their own
expense with horse, arms, and accoutrements, and they
were to be ordered, placed, and disposed as the governor
saw fit in lieu of the force in the Cherokee nation. Service
was for six months with the garrisons and Rangers being
paid on a monthly basis every three months while the 50
men in the "standby troop" were to be paid at the end of
any expedition they were sent on. A bounty of 30 pounds
was to be paid for the scalp of any warrior killed in battle.

Although the Creeks, Yamasees, and Choctaws had yet to
sign peace treaties, the combination of frontier forts and
Rangers prevented any major attacks. Minor raids still
occurred from time to time; even after negotiations with
the Creeks began in October 1717, the peace was an uneasy
one. The "standby troop" was continued by an act of 1718
and the governor was authorized to increase it should the
occasion warrant. The Rangers were disbanded (hereafter
no mention will be made of the Rangers unless they were
acting as scouts or light horse in conjunction with other
troops).

There were threats of a Spanish invasion in 1719 and a
small force was sent to spy on the activities at St. Augustine

and to attack the Yamasees in the vicinity. On receiving word of the formation of an invasion fleet, the militia was called out. A Spanish fleet, loaded with troops for an invasion of South Carolina, actually sailed but was diverted while en route. The militia remained under arms for about two weeks before being sent home. The standby troop of 50 men was disbanded shortly thereafter.

A new act was passed in 1719 enlisting trusted Negro slaves in the militia which then numbered about 1,600 white men. Upon an alarm, the previously selected slaves were to report to the colors of their respective companies and were to be armed with a musket, hatchet or pike by the captain of that company. The number of Negroes in any one company was not to exceed the number of white men.

A bloodless revolution occurred in December 1719 when the people revolted against the Proprietors and proclaimed James Moore as governor. The town militia and a large majority of the militia in the country were on the side of the people and Governor Johnson found himself nearly helpless. In 1720 Governor Moore ordered the militia turned out on the threat of a new Spanish invasion, which again failed to materialize. When two British men-of-war came into Charles Town harbor and recognized Johnson as governor, he appointed the captain of H.M.S. *Flamborough* as the colonel of the Berkeley Regiment but the troops refused to obey him. Threats of using the five British men-of-war then in the harbor to bombard the town proved equally fruitless as the recently repaired fortifications mounted over 70 cannon and 500 men were ready to man them. Shortly thereafter (May 1721), the provisional royal governor, Francis Nicholson, arrived with a company of British soldiers and South Carolina became a royal colony.

At this time the militia numbered about 2,000 men: the Northward Regiment had twelve companies, the Southern Regiment had six companies, and there were small garrisons in the various forts. The magazine in Charles Town contained approximately 1,000 muskets without bayonets, 1,000 cartouche boxes, 240 pistols and 170 barrels of powder.

Chapter II

The Militia
Under Royal Government

In September 1721 a new militia, act, similar to the act of 1716, was passed. Company musters and drills were still to be held every two months but battalion drills of two or more companies were to be held once a year, replacing the regimental drill. The colony was spreading out geographically, and with only two regiments of foot, the distances some of the companies had to travel to join their regiment were considerable.

The year 1727 was one of both internal and external difficulties. The Commons House and people refused to cooperate with the acting governor, Arthur Middleton, and wanted to pay the expenses of the province by issuing bills of credit (paper money) rather than by paying taxes; the Northward Regiment had to be ordered to disband when 250 armed men from it threatened the Council. The Yamasees and Lower Creeks were raiding the outlying settlements, and expeditions against each tribe were authorized in September. In Granville County, a temporary regiment (or in modern-day parlance, a task force) was formed of contingents from two companies from the Berkeley Regiment and five from the Colleton Regiment. It was disbanded early in the following year.

An expedition was sent against the Yamasees in February 1728 which not only defeated the Indians but also humiliated the Spaniards who did nothing to aid their allies. This victory had a tremendous effect on all the southern Indians, and the planned expedition against the Lower Creeks was cancelled when negotiations with that nation were completed on very favorable terms for South Carolina.

Conflict between the acting governor and the Commons House continued and no legislation was enacted until eight months after the arrival of Governor Robert Johnson in December 1730. According to the historian McCrady, the white population of the province was reduced from 14,000 in 1724 to 7,300 in 1734, the result of a series of natural disasters and some emigration. Using the 1 in 5 ratio, the militia strength would have decreased from 2,800 to 1,500; the latter figure would appear to be exceedingly small as Governor Johnson reported the militia of Georgia and South Carolina as numbering 3,500 in 1734.

A shipment of military stores was received in August 1731 which included 72 cannon for the fortifications and 300 each of muskets, bayonets, cartouche boxes, and swords, as well as 50 pole axes (these were just what the name implied, an axe head on a 7-foot pole with a spearhead at the top; the number would indicate that these were intended as fighting weapons and not as halberds to be carried by sergeants of the foot regiments as a badge of rank).

In November 1732 the first group of Swiss colonists arrived for the new township of Purrysburg which was located on the east bank of the Savannah River about 30 miles above its mouth. Ultimately several hundred Swiss followed and a Swiss regiment was formed in the township; by 1735 twenty commissions had been issued for this new regiment.

General James Oglethorpe arrived in Charles Town in January 1733 with the first group of settlers for the new colony of Georgia. They continued by ship to Port Royal where they were temporarily housed in the recently completed barracks. The Georgia colony was established on the land between the Savannah and Altamaha rivers and was to be completely independent except that the governor of South Carolina was to be in command of the Georgia militia

during alarms. The land between the Altamaha and St.
Mary's rivers was claimed by South Carolina until 1763
when it was annexed by Georgia.

By the end of 1733 regiments of foot had been established
in Craven and Granville Counties, bringing the total to five
including the Purrysburg Regiment. The latter was small
but nevertheless a nominal regiment having three field officers (a colonel, a lieutenant colonel and a major). At this
time, the Craven Regiment had four companies; the Berkeley Regiment, eleven (13 if the Charles Town companies
are included); the Colleton Regiment, eight; and the Granville Regiment, two. The Charles Town companies were,
strictly speaking, a part of the Berkeley Regiment but seem
to have enjoyed a semi-independent status for many years.
When they were reorganized into four companies in 1735,
the senior captain was promoted to major of the Berkeley
Regiment.

A new militia law was passed in 1734 but made no major
changes to the law of 1721. The patrol act of 1734 called for
a patrol captain and four men in the district of each militia
company (Charles Town had two such patrols of a patrol
captain and eight men each) who were to visit every plantation at least once a month. Each man was to have a good
horse and be equipped with one pistol, a carbine or musket,
a cutlass and a cartridge box with at least twelve cartridges.
Such patrols were paid and were exempt from militia duty
and muster while so serving. Their duties were to take up
any slave found outside the bounds of his master's land
without a ticket, or permit, and to search Negro houses for
weapons or stolen goods.

An inventory of small arms in the armory in 1735 included 260 muskets, 300 each of bayonets, cartouche boxes
and cutlasses, 100 hand bills (a hook-shaped weapon,
mounted on a 7-foot wooden shaft, sharpened on the con-
cave side, with a spike on the opposite side and a spearhead
at the end of the shaft) and 50 pole axes. The last two
weapons had long been obsolete and were probably supplied

by the crown from the supply in the Tower of London.
(Bows and arrows had been furnished to the colony of
Massachusetts during its early days!) In addition, the "armory over the council chamber" contained nearly 600 muskets,
140 pistols and 450 cartouche boxes, most of which needed
repair.

The three companies in the new townships of Orangeburg,
Amelia, and Saxe-Gotha were placed under the command of
a major in March 1736 but were not included in any of the
regiments. By 1737 the Craven, Colleton, and Granville
regiments had each added one new company.

When reports were received early in February 1737 of a
possible Spanish invasion, a force of 100 men was raised and
sent to Port Royal under the command of the colonel of the
Colleton Regiment; it was doubled by the end of the month
and increased to 270 men on March 19. However, when no
unusual activity was reported at either Cuba or St. Augustine, it was reduced to 100 men, who were finally discharged
on May 21.

In September 1738 the Charles Town companies were
reorganized into a new regiment of six companies of 100
men each. Six weeks later when the new regiment drilled
and passed in review with their colors flying, the 29 officers
were "all dressed in scarlet in regimental uniformity." There
is evidence that many of the well-to-do officers in the other
regiments were also wearing scarlet uniforms at this time,
particularly in the low country. General Oglethorpe's newly
raised 42nd Regiment of Foot came into Charles Town
harbor in October on its way to Georgia. Except for the
possibility of small detachments being stationed in forts on
the Savannah River, the 42nd Regiment never served in
South Carolina.

Inasmuch as there is much confusion concerning the
organization of British and colonial regiments, as well as
the terms "regiment" and "battalion," an explanation is in
order.

The South Carolina militia during most of its early history was organized into regiments (normally on a geographical basis) with a colonel as the commanding officer, assisted by a lieutenant colonel and a major. Each of the several companies in a regiment was commanded by a captain, assisted by a lieutenant and an ensign. Regimental musters were held once a year until 1721 when subdivisions of a regiment, consisting of two or more companies, became highly desirable because of the increase in the regimental area as the province expanded. The militia act of 1738 reinstated the requirement of a regimental muster once a year but was amended by the act of 1739 to require battalion musters of three or more companies instead. This new subdivision in the South Carolina militia regiments of foot was a direct result of companies being formed in newly settled areas and being included in an existing regiment, rather than being classed as independent companies until new regiments were formed.

Each British regiment had a proprietary colonel who received the pay and other benefits but did not actually command the regiment in the field. While a regiment was frequently identified by the name of the proprietary colonel, it was commanded by a lieutenant colonel who was assisted by a major; both of these field officers were captains of companies as well, receiving the pay of both ranks. The lieutenant colonel commanded the grenadier company of the regiment and the lieutenant in his company was given the title of captain-lieutenant (which meant he received the pay of a lieutenant but did the work of a captain as the lieutenant colonel probably left the administration of the company to him). In many instances, a regiment had more than one battalion, each commanded by a lieutenant colonel and each the equivalent of a one battalion regiment; thus, when two battalions of a British regiment served together, they would be the equivalent of a brigade of two regiments whereas two (or more) battalions of an American regiment would be only one regiment.

General Oglethorpe was the proprietary colonel of the 42nd Foot but Lieutenant Colonel William Cook commanded the regiment. When Oglethorpe exercised command of the regiment, it was in his capacity as general and/or governor, i.e., Captain-General in command of all the forces present.

The governor at St. Augustine in 1738 proclaimed that all slaves escaping from the English colonies would be given their freedom on arriving in Spanish-controlled territory. Word of this proclamation was circulated among the slaves in South Carolina. In September 1739 a group of about 20 slaves at Stono broke into a warehouse and, after arming themselves with muskets and ammunition, set out for Florida, killing, burning and looting as they went. Their number had grown to about 60 when the local militia companies succeeded in blocking their escape route and killed or captured the majority; total fatalities for the day were about 20 white and 44 Negroes, the greater part of the former having been killed during the surprise attacks before the alarm was sounded. Some of the Negroes who escaped and returned to their plantations were identified and executed.

As a result of a Spanish raid on Amelia Island in Georgia in late 1739, Oglethorpe sent a retaliatory force into Florida which "swept down to the gates of St. Augustine" before withdrawing to the St. John's River. Finding so little reaction to his raid, Oglethorpe began correspondence with South Carolina in an effort to form a joint expedition to capture St. Augustine and all of Spanish Florida.

South Carolina was reluctant to provide the size force Oglethorpe wanted because its population had been reduced by smallpox in 1737 and 1738 and yellow fever in 1739. There was also the possibility of further slave uprisings. However, after Oglethorpe came to Charles Town on March 23 and agreed to a smaller force, a bill was enacted on April 5, 1740, authorizing the raising of a provincial regiment, and providing supplies and ships to be sent on the St. Augustine expedition. However, this expedition was unsuccessful.

On June 28, 1742, a Spanish fleet appeared off St. Simon's Island and put a large force ashore on July 5. A request for assistance had been sent to Charles Town when the fleet first appeared and Lieutenant Governor Bull responded by putting the militia on a standby alert and impressing, arming and manning seven ships with 70 cannon, 68 swivels, 575 muskets, and over 600 men. The senior commanding officer of the British men-of-war in Charles Town harbor delayed the sailing of the fleet for a week after the South Carolina ships were reported ready, and on their arrival at St. Simon's Island, it was found that the Spanish troops and fleet had withdrawn only a day or so before.

Lieutenant Governor Bull, in a letter to H. M. Council, in September 1742, reported that there were not over 4,000 men in the South Carolina militia, scattered in an area extending 200 miles along the coast and 150 miles inland, so that 2,000 could not be gathered in less than a week.

General Oglethorpe made another attempt to capture St. Augustine in 1743 but South Carolina refused to furnish troops in view of his erratic and futile performance as a field commander in 1740.

The militia act of 1747 limited the governor's use of the militia to within the boundaries of South Carolina and then only in times of insurrection, rebellion, or invasion. This act was continued and/or revived until 1778 and was still in effect during the first three years of the Revolutionary War. The sections on arms and accoutrements, musters, and battalion drills remained essentially unchanged. New administrative sections were added including the requirement that in cases where a company was ordered to march out of its own county, the names of all men in the company were to be written on slips of paper, placed in a hat and shaken, and the required number (not to exceed three-quarters of those enrolled) was to be drawn out at random to determine

who should go. Another new section provided that all the
militia companies on James Island and in the Charles Town
Regiment were to be exercised in the use of cannon twice a
year.

Trusted Negro slaves could be enlisted in companies outside of Charles Town, not to exceed one-third the number
of white men in the company, and in Charles Town, the
total number enlisted was not to exceed one-half the total
number of male slaves in the town. In time of alarm, they
were to be armed by their masters with a good musket, a
hatchet, a powder horn and a shot pouch with ammunition
enough for 20 rounds, and six spare flints. Any slave, or
white indentured servant, who killed or captured one enemy
or captured any enemy colors was to be granted his freedom.
Any slave who conducted himself bravely in battle, but to
a lesser degree, was to be given, each and every year thereafter, a livery coat and breeches of good red Negro cloth,
turned up with blue, and a black hat and a black pair of
shoes.

With the dwindling of the population of Purrysburg during the late 1730s, the Swiss Regiment gradually was reduced
to no more than a township company and by 1741 was included as one of the companies in the Granville Regiment.
Two of the original Swiss officers were the lieutenant
colonel of the Granville Regiment and captain of the Purrysburg Company at this latter date. On the other hand, the rest
of the townships and outlying settlements increased in population and their militia companies with them. When the
townships were first established, it was the intention of the
lieutenant governor to form a new regiment of the militia
companies of New Windsor, Orangeburg, Amelia, Saxe-
Gotha, and Fredericksburg and any adjoining settlements
(a span of about 100 miles). As it actually developed, however, the inhabitants were taken into the regiments of the
counties in which they resided. The Saxe-Gotha Company
which had men on both sides of the Congaree River was
dismembered with those on the east bank going into the

Craven Regiment and those on the west into the Berkeley Regiment.

Craven, the largest of the counties (its southern boundary was the Santee - Congaree - Saluda River line), thought nothing of distance and took the new companies into its regiment as soon as they were formed. The Berkeley, Colleton, and Granville regiments seemed to place the new companies in a sort of "limbo" for some time, acknowledging their existence but because of the distances involved not regarding them as an integral part of the regiment. For example, in 1742 commissions were made out for the officers of two new companies in the Welsh Tract as being in the Craven County Regiment but the commissions for the officers "of a place called 96 down to Saludy in the out part of the province" were for an independent company.

The companies in Orangeburg, Amelia, and Saxe-Gotha had been under the command of a major since 1736. By 1753 this independent battalion had increased to seven companies, with four of the upper companies listed in the Berkeley Regiment as the Township Battalion under their own major. Two years later the seven companies had become a full-fledged regiment of foot whose beats included much of the area between the Edisto and the Saluda-Congaree rivers, almost as far west as Ninety Six.

After the militia returns were submitted in May 1757, two new companies on the Savannah River and one company at New Windsor were added to this regiment. Its official designation at this date was the Regiment in the Upper Parts of Berkeley County but it was later known as the Orangeburg Regiment.

Another new regiment of foot was formed in the area of the Welsh Tract and upper Queensboro township by 1755. The following year the inhabitants of the Peedee petitioned the governor to remove the colonel from command and he was succeeded by the lieutenant colonel, who was promoted in 1757. This, obviously, was the Welsh Tract Regiment, sometimes known as the Peedee Regiment and ultimately as the Cheraws Regiment.

Following the receipt of the militia returns in May 1757, and the division by the Council of oversized companies to form additional companies, the regiments of foot were organized as given in Table 1. In times of invasion or attack, the strength of the militia could be increased with the trusted Negro slaves and alarm men. The latter were certain public officials, former militia officers with more than ten years service as captain or higher rank, the clergy, the infirm, those over 60, etc., who were excused from attending routine musters and drills by the militia act, but who were required to "attend under the colours of the company in the district in which such person shall actually live, completely armed and furnished as is directed for the foot soldier," in case of an actual alarm.

The 8th Regiment of Foot was established in November 1758 from existing companies of the Craven Regiment in the area northwest of Williamsburg township between the Saluda-Congaree and Lynches rivers, extending northward to the Waxhaws. It originally consisted of seven or eight companies in the new St. Marks Parish and was at first identified as the St. Marks Regiment; later it was known as the Camden Regiment.

TABLE 1

REGIMENT	OFFICERS AND MEN	COMPANIES
Charles Town	775	6
Berkeley County	782	12
Colleton County	698	11
Craven County	1,870	30
Granville County	432	7
Welsh Tract	829	14
Upper Berkeley	717	12
(7 regiments)	6,123	92

Aside from general dissatisfaction with the South Carolina Indian trade and intrusion on Indian lands, the principal cause of the Cherokee War was the killing of approximately 30 Cherokees in Virginia in 1758, as the Indians were returning home from General Forbes' expedition which had captured Fort Duquesne. Governor Lyttelton attempted to placate the Cherokees with presents but some of the hotheads set out for Virginia while others raided the settlements in the South Carolina backcountry in April 1759. After the initial raids, relative calm prevailed but reports and rumors persisted of Indian insolence and plans for attacks. In September the traders were ordered out of one of the more truculent Cherokee towns by Charles Town and an embargo declared on all arms and ammunition to the Cherokee nation. More scalping raids followed and both forts in the Cherokee Nation were isolated.

On October 1, 1759, the Orangeburg, Camden, and Cheraw regiments were ordered to muster their companies and draft half of their number to be on notice to march with two commissioned officers for each company and one field officer for each regiment. Five days later the governor alerted the detachments of Independents and Provincials in or near town, and notified the colonels of the Charles Town, Craven, Colleton, Granville, and Berkeley regiments to muster all their companies to draft half their men to be ready to march. Half of the Regiment of Horse, a number of volunteers from the Artillery Company, and a company of gentlemen volunteers on horseback were to accompany the expedition which was to number 1,500 men, exclusive of Catawbas and Chichasaws who had also been alerted.

Among the eight officers comprising the governor's staff for the expedition was William Drayton, an aide-de-camp. There is a portrait by Jeremiah Theus which identifies the subject as a Drayton and shows him dressed in the elaborate uniform of a Hussar, or light cavalryman. It was the custom of the time for prominent military personages to dress their aides (or even orderlies) in Hussar uniforms of their own design and quite likely this painting is of William Drayton in the uniform of Aide to the Governor. The Hussar cap is black fur with a red bag ending in a gold tassel. The jacket is light blue with three vertical rows of gilt buttons and a dozen or more horizontal rows of gold lace across the front in line with the buttons. The pelisse (decorative overjacket, normally worn hung over the left shoulder) is red and has gilt buttons and dark fur lining and edgings. The breeches are red, and there is a blue and gold sash or girdle.

Two large delegations of Cherokees arrived in town to confer with the governor in regard to settling the grievances of both sides and restoring trade. The governor was determined to proceed with the expedition and told the Indians a treaty would be signed in the Cherokee nation on his terms. The expedition set out late in October, accompanied by the Cherokees under guard for "their own protection." Another delegation of Cherokee head men met the governor at Amelia and were likewise "given protection" but kept separated from the original delegation. On rendezvousing at the Congarees, it was found that the expedition numbered only about 1,000 men. As the Charles Town Regiment had taken over the duties in town normally performed by the Independents and Provincials, a draft of 500 additional men was ordered from the other seven regiments.

The army on the march in November is described as being a column two miles long in the following order: (1) advance guard under a lieutenant from the Independents, (2) Regiment of horse, (3) volunteer light horse, (4) artillery company with the field pieces and ammunition carts, (5) the governor and his staff, (6) Independent and Provincial companies, (7) Camden Battalion, (8) Cheraw Battalion, (9) Indian hostages under guard, (10) rear guard, and (11) 100 wagons and carts, pack horses, and servants under a strong guard of militia. After rejoining the Orangeburg Battalion which had gone on ahead of the army to Saluda Old Town, the army totaled 1,687 men, of whom only 1,300 could be classed as fighting men.

Companies and small detachments were continuously join-
ing the army but as the *Gazette* reported, "the rifle-barrel
men" (backcountry men, armed with rifles) continued to
desert (ten or twelve a day); it should be noted, however,
that the muster rolls show a proportionate number of low-
country men who "were evidently lost in the mountains"
but managed to find their way home. When the army arrived at Ninety Six, a week was spent building a stockade
(90 feet on a side) around Mr. Grundy's barn, which was
used as a storehouse for provisions.

After leaving Ninety Six with a troop of Rangers scouting
ahead and on the flanks, the army arrived at Fort Prince
George on December 9 without incident. The army had
practiced deploying into line of battle on both sides of
the road prior to reaching Twelve Mile Creek where an
expected ambush failed to materialize. The men of the
detachments from the Berkeley, Granville, and Colleton
regiments arrived while negotiations were in progress, and
shortly thereafter a treaty was signed wherein the Cherokees
agreed to deliver the Indians who had killed the South
Carolinians. Most of the Indian hostages were released,
about 28 being retained at Fort Prince George to be ex-
changed individually as the killers were brought in. As
smallpox spread through the camp, the triumphant army
deserted in droves and Lyttelton gave the order to return
to the settlements.

Although the militia took no part in the two campaigns
against the Cherokee nation in 1760 and 1761, the companies on the frontiers were pursuing small scalping parties
or fighting for their lives in the numerous private forts
where the settlers gathered.

Seven companies of 75 Rangers each were authorized in
February 1760 but only partly raised at that time; any force
of Rangers, of course, came from the militia of the back-
country, either as volunteers or by being drafted. In April,
all seven companies were raised but not to full strength.
Some were ranging on the frontiers while the majority

assembled at Ninety Six for a sweep to Fort Prince George. The latter were dispersed for about a month to await the arrival of Colonel Montgomery's troops before reassembling at full strength. On June 28, when Montgomery departed from Ninety Six for Fort Prince George, 385 Rangers were a part of his army, performing the functions of light cavalry, i.e., scouting ahead and protecting the flanks and rear of the main body.

Following the withdrawal of Montgomery, some of the Rangers were reduced with the remainder ranging on the frontiers. In September 1760, the seven companies were again completed to full strength and a major commandant appointed to command them. The following month, 269 Rangers took supplies into Fort Prince George, carrying jerked beef from 26 cattle on their saddles and 2,550 pounds of flour on 22 pack horses. In November, all seven companies of Rangers, totaling 459 men, assembled at Ninety Six and the fort was again supplied by Rangers driving 75 cattle and escorting seven wagons containing flour, salt, tools for repairing the fort, and clothing. This time the Rangers stayed long enough to repair the fort and stock it with firewood.

In January 1761 Lieutenant Governor Bull told the Commons House that as the Rangers were up to full strength, he wanted provision made for an adjutant and a quartermaster and to add one or two troops to the seven already existing. He then mentioned that he had ordered a cheap uniform for the private men (Rangers) suitable to their duty, but he gives no description. If any such uniforms were actually supplied, they were probably oznaburg hunting shirts and hats such as were provided the two regiments of riflemen (later the 5th and 6th South Carolina Regiments of the Continental Line) when they were raised in 1776.

The Rangers numbered 550 men in February when Fort Prince George was resupplied with 85 cattle, 95 hogs, 14 wagon loads of flour and four more of trade goods. The latter were to be used to buy back the captives held by the

Cherokees, including 47 Independents and 35 Provincials from the Fort Loudoun Garrison.

When Grant's expedition reached Ninety Six in May, 400 Rangers were added to it with the rest "scouring" the southwest frontier to protect its flanks as it entered the Cherokee nation. When Grant's forces withdrew in October after the peace treaty was signed, the Rangers were reduced to four companies. The last two companies were discharged in July 1762.

The years following the Cherokee Wars were essentially peaceful except for raids by the Creeks late in 1763. The threat of a new Cherokee war in 1771–72 did not materialize. There were numerous grand jury reports on the ruinous state of the fortifications and of the failure to enforce the patrol and militia laws. The Regulator movement in South Carolina in 1767–69 did not result in armed confrontation and conflict as in North Carolina, but several high-ranking militia officers had their commissions revoked for either being Regulators or for failing to act against them. The colonel of the Cheraw Regiment resigned his commission (it was not accepted) when several companies refused to aid in the arrest of some Regulators.

The number of regiments of foot was increased to nine when the Saluda Regiment was raised in the "Dutch Fork" (the area between the Broad and Saluda rivers) in 1764. The Ninety Six Regiment was formed in 1767 between the Saluda and Savannah rivers, above New Windsor and Saxe-Gotha, from the inhabitants of the existing settlements and the new townships of Londonborough, Hillsborough, Boonesborough, and Belfast. The regiment in the New Acquisition or New District (ceded by North Carolina in 1772) was established in 1773. The twelfth was formed in 1774 when the Saluda Regiment was divided into two regiments, the Enoree River being the line of demarcation between the Forks of the Saluda and the Upper Saluda regiments. The strength of the militia is estimated to have been 14,000 men in 1774.

There is no existing evidence that indicates uniformed companies in the militia outside of the Charles Town Regiment, the Regiment of Horse, the Artillery Company, and the two Provincial Regiments of 1757 and 1760. There is a good deal of evidence, however, to indicate that many of the militia officers in the regiments of foot wore scarlet uniforms. A portrait by Theus painted prior to 1775 shows the lieutenant colonel of the Craven Regiment in a scarlet uniform with black facings, flat gilt or brass buttons, and a black cocked hat edged with gold lace. It is possible that black was the facing color for all South Carolina militia regiments as such uniforms were reported outside of the Charles Town Regiment in the early years of the Revolution.

Chapter III

The Regiment of Horse

The militia act of 1696 authorized the governor to raise one or more troops of horse as he saw fit. The members of the "Troop" were to furnish their own horses, arms, accoutrements and horse furniture and were required to live within five miles of the rendezvous or within an hour's ride of it. Subsequent sources refer to the Troop as the Governor's Life Guards or Horse Guards. In view of mention of the Governor's Life Guards as early as 1672 and of the use of horses on an expedition against the Indians in 1673 (and the loss of all of the militia acts prior to 1696), it is quite probable that the Troop of Horse was in existence for many years prior to this act. The phraseology "to raise one or more troops of horse" is used consistently in the militia acts until the American Revolution, so the use of those words in the act of 1696 does not necessarily imply the initial raising of the Troop.

By 1700 the officers of the Troop were wearing scarlet uniforms, and according to John Lawson, the Troop was not only well disciplined but also was the best in America, being composed mostly of gentlemen and well mounted.

In 1701 an unsuccessful attempt was made to establish a troop of horse on a full time basis: "That 30 men have 5 pounds per annum to be in readiness with horse, arms, and ammunition to go after runaways or against Indians if occasion and to be paid for every day they are upon service . . . be accutered with saddle and arms at ye charge of the

26

public . . . and shall be exempt from serving in ye militia."
It seems improbable that this was intended to affect the
Troop already in existence but instead to raise a second
troop similar to the future Rangers. A similarly unsuccessful attempt was made in January 1702 "to pay 20 men and
horse, in arms to be placed at such places as shall be
thought most convenient for ye security of ye country."

One or more troops of horse were again authorized by the
militia act of 1703 but no limit of distance from the rendezvous was mentioned. The "gentlemen troopers" after being
accepted by the colonel of the Troop were exempt from service in the foot militia but were required to furnish their
own arms, horse, and furniture, all of which had to be approved by the colonel. Here one can see the formation of
an "elite" military organization, exclusive in nature and
composed of gentlemen volunteers who were rich enough
to provide their own horses, arms, equippage and uniforms.
It was a small group of horsemen, commanded by a colonel,
and clearly patterned after the three British Troops of Life
Guards; quite possibly their scarlet uniforms were lined and
cuffed with blue like those of the English First Troop.

Contemporary accounts of the French and Spanish invasion of the province in 1706 mention the gentlemen of
the Troop, commanded by their colonel, riding into Charles
Town the day the ships were sighted. In 1708 the strength
of the Governor's Troop of Horse Guards was reported to
be 45 officers and men. It was part of the force under
Governor Charles Craven that stopped the advance of the
Yamasees in 1715 near the head of the Combahee River
and turned them back. The militia act of 1716 again
authorized the governor to raise one or more troops of
horse as he saw fit.

In June 1721 the provisional royal governor, Francis
Nicholson, issued commissions to the colonel, lieutenant-
colonel, and major of the Troop and blank commissions
for the captain, lieutenant, and cornet (the lowest rank
commissioned officer of cavalry, equivalent to an ensign or

S. C. REGIMENT OF HORSE: (LEFT) TROOPER, 1756; (RIGHT) TROOPER, 1740.

second lieutenant of infantry). The latter three officers were to be appointed by the colonel.

The militia act of 1721 not only authorized the governor to raise one or more troops of horse as he saw fit, but also to raise one or more troops of dragoons, "who shall be armed with their fuzees [light weight muskets] slung, and in all other respects as the foot companies are, only that they shall be provided with horses." The term dragoon originally applied to a mounted infantryman who used his horse for rapid transportation but who dismounted and fought on foot when he got to the scene of action. There is no evidence that dragoons were ever raised under this act or the act of 1734 which was identical. There was no mention of dragoons in any of the later militia acts.

The Troop was apparently armed with only swords and pistols until 1736 when carbines were added to the equipment. [At this date, martial music was provided by trumpets and kettledrums.] It mustered every two months according to the militia law and also paraded on ceremonial occasions with the Charles Town companies. When delegations of Indian chiefs arrived to confer with the governor, the Troop customarily met them at some distance and escorted them into town. In 1738 a minimum height of 14 hands was established for all the horses ridden by the troopers.

A second Troop in the regiment was raised in Stono in April 1739. It received its arms, uniforms, and horse furniture the following January. The uniform of the first Troop at this time (and presumably that of the second also, as the regiment was "uniformly cloathed") is described as follows: a mazarine blue broadcloth cloak and coat, the coat lined with scarlet, with white metal (silver colored) buttons about the size of an English shilling and slashed sleeves; scarlet waistcoat and breeches; a broadsword with a half-basket hilt; close silver-laced hats, not less than an inch wide on the outside, cockades, top gloves and queue wigs. There were also blue broadcloth saddle housings and

holster caps with a blue fringe, a full curb bridle trimmed
with white, and shoeboots.

A third Troop was raised in Craven County in February
1740 (it was still in existence in July 1744 but seems to have
been disbanded prior to July 1750). In 1742 the colonel
of the regiment pointed out that the militia act empowered
him "to direct and appoint what shall be the cloathes and
accoutrements of the same, in order therefore that the
several troops in the said regiment should be uniform for
the more decent appearance of the same." He described
the uniform as follows: mazarine blue cloth coats, double
breasted, with brass buttons and slashed sleeves; short red
waistcoats with brass buttons; buckskin breeches, boots and
spurs; gold-laced hats with cockades and brown bob wigs;
horseman's swords, carbines fitted for a swivel, cross buff
belts; curb bridles, blue housings and holster caps, blue
cloaks, and bay horses not less than 14 hands high with tail
pieces. The listing of the cloaks with the horse furniture
would seem to indicate that they would be rolled and fas-
tened to the rear of the saddle when not being worn.

When a Spanish invasion was threatened in July 1742, the
Charles Town Troop escorted the lieutenant governor to
Port Royal. In March 1743, a fourth Troop was raised in
St. George Parish. In the "plan for the defence in case of
invasion" drawn up in April 1743, the Berkeley County
(Charles Town) Troop of Horse was to mount and attend
the lieutenant governor, unless otherwise directed, while
the Colleton County (Stono), Craven County, and Dor-
chester (St. George's) Troops were to mount and rendezvous
at Pon Pon Bridge and await further orders.

In July 1744 the declaration of war with France was
proclaimed in Charles Town with pomp, ceremony, and a
display of military force to impress a delegation of Creeks.
The Charles Town Regiment of Foot was drawn up in two
columns facing each other with the Craven and St. George's
Troops of Horse Guards at one end of the columns and the
Charles Town and Stono Troops of Horse Guards at the

other. The dignitaries of the province then assembled, and after the first reading of the proclamation at the Council Chamber, the regiments and dignitaries slowly marched off toward the fortifications with the trumpets and French horns of the mounted troops sounding "Britain Strike Home," alternating with the drums of the foot soldiers beating "The Grenadiers March." The proclamation was again read at the batteries and salutes fired by the cannon in the fortifications and ships in the harbor. In July 1750 Governor Glen in a letter to the Lords Commissioners for Trade and Plantation wrote, "There is in this province a Regiment of Horse Militia consisting of three Troops, they are all regularly armed with carbines, pistols and broad swords, uniformly clothed in blue, with buff shoulder belts, etc., and mounted on bay [dark reddish brown] horses. They are always appointed to meet and escort the Indians coming to Charles Town. . . ." A more complete description of this uniform was published in the *South Carolina Gazette* somewhat later: a double-breasted blue broadcloth coat with slashed sleeves, lined with red, and with gilt buttons; a red cloth waistcoat with gilt buttons and blue cloth breeches; a brown bag wig and a gold-laced hat with a black cockade; a black ribbon around the neck, leather boots, a pair of spurs and buckskin gloves; a bay horse at least 14 hands high with blue housings and holster caps; a good pair of pistols, crossbelts, a broadsword and a carbine, with bucket and proper straps; a curb bridle, breastplate (a part of the harness, not armor for the rider), crouper and tail case; and a blue cloak.

In 1756 the uniform was changed as follows: "Notice is hereby given to all the officers and private gentlemen in the Regiment of Horse under the command of the Hon. William Bull, Esq.: That the uniform clothing is regulated in the following manner, viz. All the coats and breeches to continue of the same color as at present but to be lapelled with buff colored cloth, buff colored lining and waistcoats: In which dress they are to appear in Charles Town on His

Majesty's Birthday, being the 10th day of November next."
This order simply changed the facing color from red to buff
and did not affect the remainder of the clothing and accoutrements. In May 1757 the regiment numbered 115 officers and men.

Prior to a regimental review by the governor in 1757, the
individual troops scheduled extra meetings a day or so
ahead to have "linking reins" fitted to their bridles for the
review. This may be interpreted to mean that the regiment
was prepared to fight on foot, using their carbines, like
dragoons were originally intended to do. Certain men would
be designated as "horse-holders" and lead the unmounted
horses by the linking reins to a safe place out of the line
of fire if possible. [In the British dragoons of 1715, every
tenth man would be a horse-holder; during the American
Civil War, both sides frequently used every fourth man as
horse-holder.]

In October 1759 half of the officers and men in all three
troops were called out under the command of their major
to go on Governor Lyttelton's expedition to the Cherokee
nation. A group of gentlemen volunteers, on horseback,
were organized as a troop of light horse and were to act in
conjunction with the Regiment of Horse. After the Cherokee's signed the treaty at Fort Prince George, the regiment
escorted the governor back to Charles Town, arriving early
in January 1761. While there was no actual fighting, the
500-mile march, lasting over two months, and partly under
expectation of hostile attack, provided some real soldiering
for the gentlemen troopers.

In June 1760 the Regiment of Horse was once again increased to four troops when a new troop was raised in St.
Johns Parish, Berkeley County, by the officer who had
commanded the troop of volunteer light horse on Lyttelton's
expedition.

In April 1761 the uniform was changed to the following:
a blue cloth coat with flat yellow gilt buttons, lined with

crimson cloth, and cuffed and lapelled with crimson shag; crimson shag waistcoat with flat yellow gilt buttons, blue breeches and a gold-laced hat (the officers' dress was to be the same as the privates except for gold lace on the waistcoats and other parts of the dress as usual) ; also a good bay horse not less than 14 hands high, with a bridle, saddle and blue cloth housings and pistol (holster) caps with a blue fringe; a good pair of pistols, a carbine, and a horseman's sword. This uniform was worn by the Charles Town troop when it escorted the governor to Augusta in October 1763 to a meeting of the four southern governors with the head men of the southern Indian tribes.

The Regiment of Horse continued until 1775 when it seems to disappear from history at the time its colonel became the colonel of the new Second South Carolina Regiment. Possibly, it simply disintegrated from the divisive politics of the times.

Chapter IV

The Volunteer Companies

The Artillery Company

In August 1756 consideration was given to raising an artillery company of 60 men and three officers from the ranks of the Charles Town Regiment, on the same basis as the Troops of Horse, i.e., gentlemen volunteers who could afford to buy uniforms and accoutrements. A petition for the formation of the artillery company was approved by the governor in February 1757 and the new company commenced drilling twice a month with both small arms and cannon. The uniform is described as blue broadcloth coatees, lapelled and cuffed with crimson, gilt buttons, crimson waistcoats, blue breeches, white stockings, and gold-laced hats. The officers uniform was the same except their lapels and cuffs were crimson velvet instead of broadcloth.

A detachment of the Artillery Company, consisting of the captain and about 20 volunteers in uniform with small brass field guns and ammunition carts, marched with Lyttelton to the Lower Cherokees in 1759. On the detachment's return in January 1760 the whole company underwent three months of intensive training by a detachment from the Royal Regiment of Artillery which had been sent to Charles Town for that purpose.

The militia act of July 1760 dealt only with the Artillery Company and made its earlier establishment official and legal. The members of the company were to be volunteers, approved by the captain, and to be exempt from service in the foot militia. This act called for a captain, a captain-lieutenant, a first and a second lieutenant, three lieutenant fire-workers, four sergeants and up to 100 private men (divided into bombardiers, gunners, and matrosses), all of whom were required to provide themselves with such uniforms, arms, and accoutrements as directed by the captain. The company was to muster not more than twelve or less than eight times a year and be drilled both with firelocks and cannon. Otherwise it was to be governed by the militia laws in the same manner as the troops of horse. In case of public service upon an alarm, an artillery chest, powder carts, and ammunition wagons were to be provided at public expense.

In addition to its regular musters and drills, the company was paraded on ceremonial occasions with the Charles Town Regiment, the Troop, and such detachments of the British army then in Charles Town. In June 1768, on the King's birthday, the company appeared "in a new and very genteel uniform"; the hat, coat, and stockings were the same as before but the waistcoat and breeches were changed to white like their British counterparts. (This was a summer uniform; blue waistcoats and breeches were worn during the winter months.) The Commons House appropriated 700 pounds for the captain of the Artillery Company to purchase two brass three-pounders with proper shot.

The company continued to be active until the Revolutionary War when it was expanded into a battalion of three companies, and it provided officers for the Continental Regiment of Artillery as well.

The Light Infantry and Grenadier Companies

The Charles Town Regiment in 1765 had a grenadier company and a light infantry company, both of which were uniformed in scarlet. However, by June 1766 the grenadier company seems to have disappeared as a uniformed organization and subsequently the light infantry did also.

MATROSS, CHARLES TOWN ARTILLERY COMPANY, 1758.

In May 1773 a new light infantry company was formed
on a volunteer basis similar to the Artillery Company with
the following uniform: short scarlet coats faced with black
Genoa velvet, the officers had gold lace and the privates
plain; white broadcloth waistcoats and breeches, black velvet stocks (around neck) and small black beaver (felt, not
fur) caps with black feathers; and a silver crescent inscribed
PRO PATRIA on the front of the cap. In June 1774 a new
volunteer company of grenadiers was formed out of the
Charles Town Regiment with the approval of the colonel.
They were also to provide their own uniforms and accoutrements. No description of the uniform is given but it was
probably scarlet to conform with the uniforms of the light
infantry company and of the officers of the seven battalion
companies.

Both of these companies were active until the Revolution
and served in the first battalion of the Charles Town Regiment during that war.

Chapter V

The Provincial Regiments

Provincial regiments were raised by special acts and were not part of the militia organization. All were patterned, to varying degrees, after the organization of the British regular regiments. Almost all of the officers held two commissions, one in the provincial regiment and a second (and older) in the militia (or in the case of one officer, in the British Army). The lieutenant colonel of the regiment of 1757 was a lieutenant in the British Independent Companies while his major was also the colonel of the Colleton County militia regiment. These regiments were, in effect, the regulars of that period.

The South Carolina Regiment of 1740 (Vander Dussen's)

An act of April 5, 1740, authorized the following forces to assist General Oglethorpe in an invasion of Florida, for a period of four months: a regiment of foot, to consist of a colonel, a lieutenant colonel, a major, five captains, eight lieutenants, eight ensigns, an adjutant, a commissary, 16 sergeants, 16 corporals, eight drummers, and 360 privates (eight companies of 50 men each); a troop of Rangers, if they could be raised in time; ships and boats, with supplies, provisions, ammunition, and presents for the Indians.

The time allowed for raising the troops (two to three weeks) did not permit raising the Rangers in the back-country but two additional companies were raised for the regiment of foot, which numbered 512 officers and men in ten companies actually taking part in the campaign. A volunteer company of 32 gentlemen, 15 trusted Negroes, and eight Indians accompanied the regiment. South Carolina also provided twelve 18-pound cannon, a shallow-draft schooner which mounted 14 carriage guns and twelve swivel guns, and 17 smaller craft. Two more companies for the regiment were in the process of being raised but were not completed in time to go on the expedition.

No provision in the act which authorized the regiment provided for uniforms and the time between authorization and departure was too short for any such quantity to have been procured, even if provided for. Nevertheless, the colonel's company was known as the grenadier company and its lieutenant had the title of captain-lieutenant (this meant the colonel ran the regiment while the captain-lieutenant did the job of company commander but only received the pay of a lieutenant).

The initial landing in Florida took place on May 9 with 220 men of the 42nd Regiment and the Highland Company, 125 men from the South Carolina Regiment, and 103 Indians simply crossing the St. John's River near its mouth. This placed them about 45 miles from St. Augustine in contrast with less than half that distance to march had they used the sloops and petiaugers on the St. John's River to land at Fort Picolata (captured by Oglethorpe in 1739).

After being joined by the remainder of the troops from Georgia and South Carolina, the campaign went from bad to worse when the original plan of attacking St. Augustine quickly from both the seaward and landward sides was not followed. Following the capture of a small fort on May 12, the campaign degenerated into much marching and counter-marching.

A second small fort was captured, but St. Augustine was not besieged until June 12. Three days later, the second small fort was recaptured by the Spanish forces with heavy

PRIVATE, S. C. PROVINCIAL REGIMENT OF 1757.

losses to the Georgians and Rangers occupying it. The naval forces departed from their station on July 5 and 11, and the Georgia troops withdrew on July 9. They were followed on July 11 by the South Carolina Regiment which remained as the rearguard to bring off the cannon and supplies.

Sirmans, in a masterpiece of laconism in his *Colonial South Carolina,* devoted one short paragraph to this campaign, starting with, "Oglethorpe's invasion of Florida was a fiasco from beginning to end," and concluding, "His handling of the invasion amazed the Spanish governor, Don Manuel de Mantiano who said, 'I cannot arrive at a comprehension of the conduct, or rules of this General'." McCrady points out that during the Highland risings in Scotland in 1745 Oglethorpe displayed leadership of the same caliber when the cavalry under his command, in hot pursuit of the fleeing Scots, was passed during the night by the mainbody of the infantry under the Duke of Cumberland.

The South Carolina Regiment of 1757 (Howarth's)

A provincial regiment, to be enlisted on the same terms as the British regiments, was authorized by an act of July 6, 1757. It was to consist of seven companies with the following personnel: a lieutenant colonel, a major, five captains, 14 lieutenants, seven ensigns, an adjutant, a quartermaster, 28 sergeants, 28 corporals, 14 drummers, 700 privates, a surgeon, and a surgeon's mate. Uniforms were to be provided with those of the noncommissioned officers and drummers to be a better grade of material than those of the privates. The two "Provincial Companies under martial Law" which had helped to build Fort Loudoun were disbanded by this act, but many of the men re-enlisted in the new regiment to serve under their old captains who continued under their earlier commissions, and thus were the two senior captains of the regiment. Thirty-one commissions were also made out for the regiment in August and September. The uniforms were ordered from London, together with 28 halberds and 14 drums, and were received sometime before July 1758.

The uniform is described as follows: Blue cloth coat, cuffed with buff-colored cloth and lined with buff-colored serge; white metal buttons, buff-colored cloth waistcoat, and breeches of blue cloth; hat with white lace and a cockade; one pair of coarse white thread stockings, and one pair of shoes.

The regiment reached a maximum strength of 500 in December 1758 following the enactment in May of that year of legislation empowering magistrates to enlist "all idle, lewd, disorderly men who have no visible means of support and all sturdy beggars." But in July 1759 the Commons House voted to provide money for only three companies, and that reduced amount only until the end of the year. One company at Port Royal during 1757–59 was engaged in building a new fort, Fort Lyttelton, and in August 1759 was ordered to march to reinforce Fort Loudoun. On arriving at Fort Prince George, the captain reported the loss of 20 men by desertion en route, and he was instructed to replace the deserters with 20 men from the garrison.

After the company arrived at Fort Loudoun in October, the Provincials were distributed in the following forts: Fort Loudoun, four officers and 100 men; Fort Prince George, one officer and 55 men; Fort Lyttelton, one sergeant and 13 men; Fort Johnson, one officer and 18 men; and Charles Town, six officers, 90 men, and a surgeon. About 100 men from the Charles Town and Fort Johnson garrisons accompanied Lyttelton on his expedition to the Lower Cherokees in 1759.

In February 1760 the Commons House continued the three companies of Provincials (this regiment had been known as "The Buffs" because of the facing color of their uniform) and authorized a regiment of foot of ten companies of 100 men each. The governor ordered that 260 suits of regimental clothing be provided for the men of the three companies of the Buffs, "to be made of blue strouds and as suitable (similar) to their present uniform as possible."

Fort Loudoun was starved into surrender on August 7, 1760, after being cut off for approximately eight months. The garrison, in spite of assurances of safe passage to Fort Prince George, was attacked after one day's march and 20 to 30 of the officers and men were killed; the rest were taken prisoner.

When the Rangers were taking supplies into Fort Prince George in November 1760, included were "30 suits of the old regiment's [the Buffs] cloathing for the soldiers there." By this time, however, the old regiment had become a part of the new one.

The South Carolina Regiment of 1760 (Middleton's)

The Commons House in February 1760 authorized a new provincial regiment of ten companies of 100 men each. Recruiting was slow and only about 100 men had been raised in time to take part in Colonel Montgomery's campaign against the Cherokees in 1760. The regiment numbered only five officers and 125 men in July.

An act was passed in August 1760 authorizing the raising of a Provincial Regiment to consist of ten companies of 100 privates each and a colonel, a lieutenant colonel, a major, seven captains, 20 lieutenants, ten ensigns, one adjutant, one quartermaster, one paymaster, 40 sergeants, 40 corporals, 20 drummers, one surgeon, and two surgeon's mates. In September commissions were made out for 40 officers in the new regiment. Both the act and the colonel's commission stated that the three companies of the earlier Provincial Regiment (the Buffs) were to be incorporated into the new regiment. A draft of the commission in the Archives has a sketch of Lieutenant Governor Bull's seal in which a crescent is prominently displayed; it is believed that this crescent was adopted as the insignia of the regiment and, as such, was

**S. C. PROVINCIAL REGIMENT OF 1760: (LEFT) VOLUNTEER;
(RIGHT) OFFICER.**

displayed on the front of light infantry caps worn by the entire regiment. The act also stated that the men raised in February 1760 by resolution of the Commons House were also to be a part of the new regiment and that the men of the new regiment were to be provided with uniforms after one month's service.

The uniform is described as "blue turned up with scarlet, made in the same manner as that of the Light Infantry [Company] of His Majesty's Royal [Scots] or First Regiment of Foot and looks extremely well." This meant the entire regiment wore blue coatees, waistcoats and breeches, white metal buttons and scarlet cuffs, lapels and coat linings, with a black light infantry-type cap (made by cutting off most of the brim of a felt hat, except for the front portion which was turned up vertically to form a false front to the cap). This, not by chance, is the uniform adopted by the 1st and 2nd South Carolina Regiments in 1775, and the presence of a silver crescent on the caps of the latter undoubtedly was influenced by the Regiment of 1760. Provision was also made for "gentlemen of character and very considerable property [who] propose to go as volunteers with Colonel Middleton's Regiment . . ." by prescribing a similar uniform in which "deep green" replaced the blue, resulting in a deep green uniform with scarlet facings and white metal buttons.

When Colonel Grant's expedition set out against the Cherokees in May 1761, the regiment numbered 689 men, most of whom had wintered at the Congarees and were "well trained and eager." The Commons House continued the regiment for six months after July 1. Approximately 35 men of the Buffs who had been captured at Fort Loudoun and recently ransomed, together with 55 more of the Buffs from the Fort Prince George garrison, were added to the regiment shortly before the expedition left Fort Prince George for the middle Cherokee settlement. At the same time, a light infantry company of 70 picked men was formed in the regiment.

Following the "Ring fight," during which the regiment defended the pack train, the expedition remained in the Cherokee nation until after the preliminary peace treaty was signed in September. In October the regiment was disbanded in the field as most of the enlistments had expired.

Chapter VI

The British
Independent Companies

Two transports arrived from England in May 1721 with an Independent Company for the defense of the province; it was ordered that the troops and their supplies be transported to Port Royal. The Independent Companies were regular British soldiers, raised as individual companies for garrison duty in both Great Britain and the colonies. Since there was no regimental organization, the crown was saved the expense of paying the field officers, i.e., the colonel, lieutenant colonel, and major. This particular company was drafted from Colonel Fielding's Regiment of Invalids (41st Foot) and consisted of three sergeants, three corporals, two drummers, and 100 privates. Governor Nicholson was the captain of the company which had two lieutenants, two ensigns, a surgeon, and a chaplain—the extra lieutenant and ensign were provided to permit the company to be employed in small detachments. The company was generally referred to as the "Invalids" in the records of the province and undoubtedly continued to wear the uniform of the 41st Foot (black cocked hats, trimmed with white lace, red coats with blue linings and cuffs, red waistcoats, and blue breeches) until 1731 or possibly as late as 1738 when General Oglethorpe's regiment (42nd Foot) was formed around it.

New woolen uniforms were issued every year with the old coats being cut down to make waistcoats and the coattails being made into breeches. Summer uniforms were made of oznaburg (a cheap but sturdy, lightweight woven material)

OFFICER, S. C. INDEPENDENT COMPANY, 1760.

1,000 yards of which were shipped over with the troops, together with 1,000 yards of cheap material for shirts, 200 pairs of stockings, and 200 pairs of shoes.

The privates of the Independent Company were armed with a musket, bayonet, and brass-hilted cutlass and carried their ammunition in a cartouche box supported by a shoulder belt and waist belt of buff leather. Sergeants carried a halberd and officers a spontoon, or half-pike; both wore swords.

Fort King George was constructed near the mouth of the Altamaha River (approximately two-thirds of the distance down the coast of Georgia) which was to be garrisoned by the Independent Company. The site was on a bluff overlooking the north bank of the river and a triangular area 200 feet by 300 feet surrounding a blockhouse was defended on two sides by mud walls and a fosse (dry ditch), palisadoed, and by a parapet of fascines (cylindrical bundles of sticks) and earth fronting on the river. Several palmetto huts and a barracks were erected in the triangular area. Temporarily manned by the militia while the Independents recovered from scurvy and became adapted to the climate, Fort King George quickly became the source of diplomatic protests by both Spain and the governor of St. Augustine.

A fire in January 1726 destroyed the barracks, some of the huts, and parts of the wooden defenses, with the total loss of provisions and tools and some of the gun carriages. The General assembly promptly authorized 2,000 pounds for provisions, supplies and temporary repairs and directed the Independent Company to continue to garrison the fort. In April 60 muskets with bayonets and cartouche boxes were sent to the garrison from the public stores, together with bullet moulds, flints, and other supplies. Whereas conditions had been far from comfortable in the fort prior to the fire, they became unbearable afterwards. A letter to the secretary of war stated that the fort contained less than one-third acre, part of it in a marsh, and was supplied only with salted provisions; also that in the past six years, four officers, one surgeon and 130 sergeants and privates had died there and many others had deserted to the Spaniards.

In the late summer of 1727, the garrison was withdrawn to Port Royal for the protection of that settlement against Spanish Indians and except for token occupation at a later date, the fort was abandoned. Part of the Independent Company was stationed in Charles Town and was paraded with the Troop of Horse Guards and the Charles Town militia companies in October 1727 when George II was proclaimed king.

Despite numerous sets of instructions from England over the years to rebuild the fort on the Altamaha and send the Independents back to garrison it, the company remained in South Carolina with its principal detachments at Port Royal and Charles Town. After instructions dated October 10, 1735, were received from England, the Independent Company departed from Port Royal for St. Simon Island in March 1736 where they were to construct a fort, and so passed from the command of the Governor of South Carolina. When Oglethorpe's 42nd Regiment of Foot was raised around the Independent Company in August 1737, the officers of that company became the senior officers of their respective ranks in the new regiment. [Oglethorpe's 42nd Foot should not be confused with the Black Watch, a Highland regiment, which was numbered the 43rd Foot when raised in 1739; it was not renumbered the 42nd until Oglethorpe's regiment was disbanded in 1749. Oglethorpe's regiment wore red uniforms with green facings while the Black Watch wore short red jackets with buff facings, Highland bonnets and kilts of the still familiar dark green, blue and black tartan.]

In August 1742 South Carolina petitioned the king for three Independent Companies to be stationed in South Carolina. Two years later, an Order in Council provided that three companies, each having one captain, two lieutenants, one ensign, four sergeants, four corporals, two drummers

and 100 privates, would be raised but to avoid transportation costs, the companies were to be recruited in the
colonies. The three captains with 60 officers and enlisted
men of the companies arrived in December 1745 in the
transport *Pelican* which also carried the arms, accoutrements and uniforms for the full complement. Some of the
officers were sent to the northern colonies to recruit the
other 279 men.

The following February, Governor Glen reported to
England that the Commons House had voted the extra pay
for the Independents and also a brick barracks was to be
built in Charles Town for them. In April 1747 he reported
that the companies were far from being completed but that
he had stationed one at Fort Frederick, Port Royal, one in
Charles Town, and the third was to be divided to garrison
Fort Johnson and Fort Moore. Some of the Independents
served as marines aboard two sloops taken into service by
the province in December 1747 to cruise for Spanish priva-
teers. They took part in the capture of one privateer.

These Independents, like the earlier company of 1721–37,
were British regulars and wore the red coats, waistcoats and
breeches; however, the color of the coatlining, cuffs, and
lapels (added for all infantry in 1743) was now Popinger
green for the Independents instead of blue, and white lace
edged the turned up brims of the black cocked hats. Arms
and accoutrements remained the same as before. Officers'
and non-commissioned officers' uniforms were scarlet; the
privates' uniforms were a brick red color because they were
made of a cheaper grade of cloth and when dyed came out
a less brilliant shade. Lace was used on the coats and waistcoats as an edging for buttonholes, pockets, and lapels. It
was silver for officers and sergeants and white for privates.
Both officers and sergeants wore crimson sashes, the sergeants' having a narrow stripe of the facing color running
the full length. Officers were further distinguished by a
silver aiguillette on the right shoulder and frequently a

gorget. Buttons were silver for officers and sergeants and pewter for privates.

In January 1748, Glen reported that he had stationed 200 of the Independents in Charles Town, housed in the brick barracks, and was using them to maintain the fortifications which otherwise would go to ruin. The third company was stationed at Port Royal. These three companies were disbanded in June and July 1749 and their places taken by three newly formed Independent Companies raised from Oglethorpe's Regiment which had been disbanded in May. A small detachment had been left at Cumberland Island, Georgia, and another detachment was sent back to Fort Frederica, also in Georgia. These new Independents continued to wear the uniform of Oglethorpe's Regiment for possibly two years until they were worn out. The *Gazette* in November 1751 mentions the fine appearance of a detachment of the three companies in their new clothing and accoutrements. The uniform of Oglethorpe's Regiment had been red with green facings but much ornamented with lace; however, the green was darker and brighter than the Popinger green facings of the Independents and has been referred to in various sources as emerald green.

In October 1753 Governor Glen set out for the Lower Cherokees with 60 men from the Independent companies and 50 laborers to build a fort on the Keowee River, which had been "solicited" by the Cherokees for seven years and which had the approval of the Crown and the South Carolina assembly. A treaty was negotiated in November deeding the area surrounding the fort site and a strip of land the width of the fort running the full distance to the Long Canes Creek settlements, and work immediately started on Fort Prince George located on the Keowee River. It was a square fort, with four bastions and a ravelin, approximately 200 feet from the corner of one bastion to another, surrounded by a dry moat; the dirt from the moat, stabilized with fascines, was used to make the earthwork walls which were surmounted by a palisade of sharp pointed wooden posts. No cannon were provided for the fort at this time but it was manned by a garrison of 16 Independents under a sergeant when Glen returned to Charles Town in December. The Independents were still furnishing detachments in Georgia, and garrisons at the Congarees, Fort Moore, Fort Frederick, and Fort Johnson, with the remainder at Charles Town.

In response to an order from the Earl of Holderness in April 1754 to send an Independent Company to assist the Virginia troops under Colonel Washington in western Pennsylvania, Governor Glen was forced to send the equivalent of a company made up of men from all three companies. This composite company joined Washington in time to take part in the defense and capitulation of Fort Necessity. The casualties of the Independent Company greatly exceeded those of the Virginians although the latter made up about two thirds of the English-American forces. It was also part of the first brigade at the battle of the Monongahela (Braddock's defeat) in 1755. In November the privates of the company were drafted into the 50th Regiment and the officers and noncommissioned officers returned to South Carolina to recruit for the three understrength companies still there. In May 1756 Governor Glen set out for the Overhill Cherokees with 90 Independents and three companies, totaling 210 Provincial troops, to build the fort long promised to that nation. The newly appointed governor, William Henry Lyttelton, arrived in Charles Town on June 1 and on the following day sent word to disband the three Provincial companies, notifying Glen of his arrival at the same time.

Governor Lyttelton reported in July 1756 that he was proceeding with the building of the fort in the Overhill Cherokee country and that he had issued six commissions for the officers of two Provincial Companies of 60 men each, who were to assist in the work. The Independent Company assigned for this task repaired Fort Prince George and installed posts in each of the four bastions for mounting a swivel gun. The dry moat was widened to 20 feet and its depth increased to seven feet; the excavated dirt was

used to build up the earthen ramparts to a height of 11 feet.
The inside was stabilized with fascines and pickets. With
all work completed by July 23, a detail of 20 men with six
pack horses was sent off to the Overhills.

The two new Provincial Companies arrived at Fort Prince
George in August, and the fort-building expedition set out
for the Overhill country near the end of September, leaving
a garrison of one ensign and 15 men of the Independent
Company. Meanwhile, during June and July, Virginia
militia had built a log fort, 105 feet square, in the Overhill
country near the site selected for the South Carolina fort
but across the Little Tennessee River. The Virginians then
returned home by way of the valley, leaving their fort without a garrison as it was intended only as a place of refuge
for the Cherokees from the French and their Indian allies.
Work was finally started on Fort Loudoun about October
15 and it was completed in July 1757, although the
elaborate system of outworks planned by De Brahm, the
engineer, was never even started. The two Provincial Companies were disbanded in August and returned to the
settlements.

The fort was a diamond-shaped earthwork with four bastions, two of which were on the low ridge at the edge of
the Little Tennessee River with the rest of the fort extending down the slope onto the valley floor. A palisade of
sharpened logs projected eight feet above the top of the
earthwork and a dry moat surrounding the fort was planted
with honey locust which grows thorns two inches long.
Twelve cannon (some of which weighed over 300 pounds),
converted from swivel guns to carriage guns by the black-
smith and carpenters, were installed on high platforms in
the bastions and two cohorns, mounted on the four-wheeled
carriages, could be used as mortars firing grenades or could
be loaded with small shot and fired level as guns. The two
acres inside the fort provided ample room for barracks,
officers' quarters, guardhouse, storehouses, magazine, a well,
and "necessary houses." The fort's normal garrison was one
company of Independents.

In October 1759 the three Independent Companies had their full complement of officers and noncommissioned officers but only 267 privates to furnish garrisons at Fort Frederica in Georgia, Fort Moore, Fort Augusta, Fort Loudoun, Fort Prince George, and Charles Town. Of these, two officers and 88 men were at Fort Loudoun and one officer and 44 men were in Fort Prince George. About 50 men from the detachment in Charles Town took part in Lyttelton's expedition of 1759.

None of the Independents participated in Colonel Montgomery's campaign of 1760 except for the garrisons in the two forts in the Cherokee nation. Montgomery returned to the coast after a firefight near Etchoe in the Middle Cherokees in which he sustained about 17 killed and 66 wounded. His force was too small to permit dividing it to leave a guard strong enough to protect the wounded and still be able to force its way through with the remainder to relieve Fort Loudoun. Its garrison of about 200 men (approximately half Independents and half Provincials), with some of their families and some traders, was starved into surernder in August 1760. Following the ransom of about 113 captives by June 1761, about 35 of the Independents were added to Grant's regulars for the campaign with 45 more from the garrison of Fort Prince George. When Grant departed for the Middle Cherokees on June 7, he left 130 invalids to garrison that fort.

At the close of the Cherokee War, the old Independents settled back into the peacetime garrison routine until December 1763 when three skeleton companies of the 60th Foot arrived to replace them. On January 14 the Independent Company in Charles Town was disbanded with 35 of its men being drafted into the 60th; the other two companies doing duty in the forts in remote parts of the province were disbanded immediately thereafter with all of their men, "who were fit," also being drafted into the 60th Foot. The officers of the Independents were placed on the half-pay list and the men who were over age or physically unfit were discharged.

Chapter VII

Other British Troops

After the wreck of H.M.S. *Loo* (the 40-gun station ship at Port Royal) on the Florida coast in February 1744, her marine detachment of 40 men under Lieutenant Vaughan was brought to Charles Town and quartered in its fortifications. In June during the alarm that followed the declaration of war with France, Governor Glen planned to take the marines to Port Royal as a part of the reinforcements for that garrison but then decided to keep them in Charles Town. Although they were ultimately reclaimed by the British Navy, they were undoubtedly the first British troops to serve in South Carolina with the exception of the Independent companies. However, they received no publicity on quartering as did the 60th and 77th Regiments in 1758, and their earlier service has gone almost unnoticed. At that date there were ten regiments of marines who wore the standard uniform of the army with only some slight modifications and were numbered not only as the 1st through the 10th Regiments of Marines but also as the 44th through the 53rd Regiments of Foot. They seem to have been partly under the army and partly under the navy, except on payday when neither the War Office nor the Admiralty wanted to pay them. In 1747 they were definitely placed under the Admiralty.

Lieutenant Hector Vaughan's detachment was from the 6th Marine Regiment (49th Foot, or Colonel Laforey's Regiment). The uniform is described as a good full-bodied

red coat, red waistcoat made from last year's coat, red
kersey breeches, and long gaiters (to above knee) made of
blue and white striped ticken. The turn-down collar, cuffs,
and coat lining were green but there were no lapels; instead,
there were six white metal buttons on each side, looped
with white lace to form "dummy" buttonholes such as
appear on lapelled coats. The headgear was a cloth grenadier cap, shaped somewhat differently from that of the
army, worn by the entire regiment. The front, including
the lower part, or little flap, was green and edged with red
lace; a crown above the king's cipher, GR, was embroidered
in red on the upper front, and the garter star was embroidered on the little flap. The upper part of the back
was red and the lower back green with the regimental
number embroidered on it.

The equipment consisted of a buff waist belt with two
black cartouche boxes, one in front and the other on the
right side; the bayonet was carried on the left side of the
waist belt. The musket was the regulation firelock used
by the army.

Both the Board of Trade in London and the British military command in the northern provinces, fearing a French-
Creek attack on Georgia and South Carolina in 1757,
ordered troops to Charles Town. Lieutenant Colonel Henry
Bouquet commanding the 1st Battalion of the Royal American Regiment (60th Foot) arrived in June with five of his
companies (400 men) and two companies of the Virginia
Provincial Regiment (200 men). The 60th Foot set up its
tents on the New Market racecourse and the Virginians were
camped outside of town as the new barracks were still under
construction. By August the rains had driven the troops into
quarters in the town and Bouquet had sent one company of
Virginians to Georgia (and contemplated sending the other
to the empty Virginia fort on the Tennessee River). Colonel
Bouquet inspected the Independents and South Carolina
militia as well as the forts and fortifications and kept his
troops busy repairing the fortifications of Charles Town.

PRIVATE, 77TH REGIMENT OF FOOT, OR MONTGOMERY'S HIGHLANDERS, 1760.

On September 1, Colonel Montgomery's Highland Battalion (77th Foot) consisting of 1,000 men in ten companies arrived in Charles Town; another new barracks for 1,000 was authorized and construction begun. In the meantime the troops had to be quartered in taverns, churches, and sheds. In February 1758, Bouquet wrote that 60th and half of the 77th Foot were provided for and the barracks for the remainder would be ready soon. The officers had to find quarters for themselves in private homes. Shortly afterwards Bouquet and the 60th departed; the two Virginia companies had returned home in January. The Highlanders remained until May 21 when they left for the northern colonies. Both the 60th and 77th Foot were to see further service in South Carolina.

The Royal American Regiment wore red uniforms (scarlet for officers and sergeants) with dark blue breeches and facings (cuffs, coat linings, and lapels). Buttons were white metal and the lace on the hats, coats, and waistcoats was silver for officers and sergeants and white for privates. Leggings were brown and belts were buff. Hats and cockades were black. "Lace," as used on a uniform, was a flat white or yellowcloth tape, about one-half inch wide, sewn on the coat and waistcoat in loops around the buttonholes, and used as edging on the hats and the pocket flaps, on the cuffs, and in some instances along the outer edges of the lapels. Although some of the regiments had plain white lace, most had one or more fine stripes of different colors woven into the lace. There were far more regiments than there were facing colors, and the variations in the different lace designs provided a distinction or a means of identifying the regiments.

The uniform of Montgomery's Regiment was short red jackets and waistcoats with dark green facings. Buttons were white metal, and lace on the coats and waistcoats was white. The bonnet was blue with black feathers and cockade. The stockings were cut from red and white checkered cloth and had a seam up the back. The belts and cartouche,

or cartridge box, were of black leather. The kilt and plaid
are thought to have been the military tartan, i.e., dark
green, blue, and black, although the grenadier company
may have had a narrow red overstripe running through the
green squares of the tartan. They were armed with muskets,
bayonets, broadswords, dirks, and claw-butted Highland
pistols.

A detachment of Royal Artillery, commanded by Lieutenant Mayne, arrived in Charles Town in December 1759
and left in April 1760; it had been sent to train the Charles
Town Artillery Company. Upon completion of the assign-
ment, it departed without taking part in Montgomery's
expedition. The uniform of the Royal Artillery was a blue
double-breasted coat with slashed sleeves and red lapels,
linings, and cuffs; a red waistcoat and red breeches; officers and sergeants wore gold lace on the coat and waistcoat and around the buttonholes, pockets, collar, cuffs and
lapels. The privates, matrosses, etc., wore yellow lace. The
lace on the waistcoats was ordered discontinued in 1759 but
may have still been worn by this detachment. Buttons were
gilt or brass. The cocked hat was black, edged with gold
lace, and had a black cockade. Stockings were white and
shoes black. Officers wore a gold aiguillette on the right
shoulder, and when under arms they also wore a gold colored gorget and crimson sash.

On April 1, 1760, Colonel Montgomery arrived by sea
with 1,200 troops, consisting of six companies of the Royal
Scots (1st Foot) and six companies of Montgomery's Highlanders (77th Foot), the latter having been in South Carolina a few years earlier. The Royal Scots were *not* a Highland Regiment but rather the oldest regiment of foot in the
British army. They were given the facetious nickname of
Pontius Pilate's Bodyguard, implying that they traced their
lineage back to the old Roman legions of early Britain.
This detachment was from the second battalion of the regiment; the first battalion was stationed in Ireland; the other

four companies of the second battalion remained in New York.

Of the six companies in South Carolina, four were "battalion," or standard companies, whereas the other two were "flank" companies—one being the grenadier company, the other the light infantry company. The coat was red (scarlet for officers and sergeants) with dark blue lapels, cuffs and coat-lining; the waistcoat was red, breeches blue, and leggins brown. White lace (silver for officers and sergeants) was on the coat and waistcoat around the buttonholes, pockets, lapels, and cuffs. Buttons were white metal. The battalion companies wore the regulation cocked hat with white lace edging and a black cockade.

The grenadiers wore a tall cloth cap: the upper front was dark blue with the King's cipher, *GR*, within the circle with the motto of the Order of St. Andrew, and the crown was gold and red; the lower front or flap was red, with the White Horse of Hanover on it and the motto, *Nec Aspera Terrent*, over it. The upper back of the cap was red, divided by white piping into three equal sectors from top to bottom, and the bottom part was blue and white figuring and a grenade with the number I on it.

The light infantry company wore a coatee (shorter than the standard coat) and a cap that was probably made by cutting the brim off of a regulation hat except in the front where it was turned up vertically to make an almost flat front for the cap. Somewhat later, light infantry caps were made of leather and were more ornate, but they were essentially the same style. The front of the cap was probably decorated with a large *GR*, a crown, and the regimental number in white or silver.

The flank companies of Montgomery's Regiment were included in the six companies in South Carolina. Nothing is known of the headgear of the light infantry company of the 77th, but the grenadier company wore a fur-fronted grenadier cap with a low red plate in the lower front and with a white *GR* and crown on it; the back had a red

SERGEANT, 60TH REGIMENT OF FOOT, OR ROYAL
AMERICANS, 1764.

upper section with white piping and a dark green bottom with a grenade with LXXVII (or possibly 77) on it. Both the grenadier and light infantry companies of all regiments wore "wings" on their coats; these were flaps of red cloth decorated with regimental lace that were sewn into the upper half of the seam where the sleeve was attached to the coat. Officers and sergeants of the flank companies of all regiments carried fusils rather than spontoons and halberds. The drummers of all regiments wore a cap similar to the grenadier cap, but not as tall, and uniforms made of the regimental facing color with red facings and much regimental lace sewn on the coats.

The troops taking part in Montgomery's expedition were the 1st and 77th, about 335 Rangers (the rest were patrolling the frontiers to protect the settlements) and about 100 of the new Provincial Regiment (only five officers and 125 men had been raised by the end of July 1760). After burning several villages and destroying the crops in the Lower Cherokees, Montgomery proceeded about 60 of the approximately 150 miles to Fort Loudoun before turning back because of the large number of wounded after a firefight of several hours near Etchoe in the Middle Cherokees. Montgomery left the four battalion companies of the Royal Scots under their own major at the Congarees and departed with the remaining eight companies, leaving the Fort Loudoun garrison to starve or surrender.

On January 6 and 8, 1761, five transports arrived in Charles Town, bringing the following troops under the command of Lieutenant Colonel James Grant: two companies of the 17th Foot, two companies of the 22nd Foot, and eight Independent Companies (newly raised in England), totaling 1,262 officers and men. He also took command of the four battalion companies of the 1st Foot, left at the Congarees by Montgomery the year before, which had recently returned to town.

No troops from the 77th Foot (with the possible exception of a few "invalids" who had been left in Fort Prince George

in 1760) took part in Grant's campaign of 1761. The popu-
lar but incorrect impression of that regiment being in South
Carolina in 1761 probably arises from the following: (a)
Grant was an officer in the 77th and had taken part in the
campaign of 1760 with that regiment, and (b) a missing
transport with 156 of Montgomery's Highlanders aboard
was reported at New Providence, and Grant sent a man-of-
war to escort it to Charles Town at the same time requesting
permission from General Amherst to use them in the forth-
coming campaign. The Highlanders (actually numbering
only 60) arrived in Charles Town late in March and set
out for Monck's Corner on April 1. About April 7, they
were ordered back to Charles Town where they embarked
for New York the week of April 11–18. Apparently Amherst
had refused Grant's request to use them.

Grant moved his troops ashore on January 12 and 13 and
started building a supply of food at the Congarees. He
blamed the delay in setting out for the Cherokees on the
lack of wagons to transport supplies, which was true to
some extent, but the transports with the heavy baggage for
his troops did not arrive in Charles Town until March 18.
Grant and his troops marched from town on March 20. In
the meantime, part of the South Carolina Regiment had
advanced to Ninety Six in February where they built a
stockade and food depot, with the wagons advancing the
food from the Congarees.

The army, when assembled at Ninety Six on May 14,
consisted of 1,400 British regulars, 689 Provincials, 401
Rangers, 57 Indians, and with wagoners and Negroes, totaled
over 2,800. The eight Independent Companies were formed
into a new British regiment, Burton's 95th Foot, after the
major assigned to the regiment arrived in Charles Town in
May with the orders for its establishment. The army
arrived at Fort Prince George on May 27 and built an ex-
tensive earthwork to protect the wagons after they were
unloaded. Six hundred pack saddles were made from the
wagon covers. The lieutenant colonel of the 95th Foot

arrived in Charles Town on May 17 and immediately set
out to join his regiment.

Grant's forces marched for the Middle Cherokees on June
7 and were attacked by the Cherokees three days later about
two miles from where Montgomery was ambushed the year
before. The Indians were driven off with Grant's casualties
amounting to eleven dead and 52 wounded. Grant left the
wounded and provisions at Etchoe with a force of 1,000
men under Middleton and marched with the remainder into
the Middle Cherokee settlements, burning 15 villages and
destroying the crops in the fields. All of the army returned
to Fort Prince George on July 9 to await a peace delegation
from the Cherokees. Part of the troops remained at the
fort rebuilding it: the rest were marched to Ninety Six
because of the necessity for hauling provisions the additional distance. The negotiations dragged on but Grant remained with his troops keeping pressure on the Cherokees.

The preliminary peace treaty was signed near Charles
Town in September and in mid-October the army began
to return to the coast leaving Fort Prince George well supplied. On December 19 the last of Grant's troops embarked,
leaving only the old Independents in South Carolina.

The 17th Foot had facings of light gray, whereas those
of the 22nd Foot were a pale, or reddish, buff color. These
two regiments each had one battalion company and one
light infantry company serving under Grant, and their uniforms were similar to those of the corresponding companies
of the 1st Foot except the breeches were red. The eight new
Independent Companies also wore a lapelled uniform with
white buttons similar to that of the battalion companies of
the 1st Foot except that the breeches and facings were red
(scarlet for officers and sergeants) and no lace was worn
on the coat and waistcoat.

Inasmuch as these companies were raised with the intention of furnishing men as replacements for any depleted or
understrength regiment in North America, a coat lining of
the proper color would produce the desired facings, and

GRENADIER, 1ST REGIMENT OF FOOT, OR ROYAL SCOTS, 1760.

the correct regimental lace could be sewn on. The facing color for Burton's Regiment was gray but it is very unlikely that the change was effected in South Carolina. However, the new field officers may have been wearing the gray facings and correct lace for the 95th Foot when they joined the regiment.

When the Independent Companies were disbanded in 1764, their places were taken by three companies of the Royal American Regiment (60th Foot). The situation was somewhat different as these companies were now under the command of Colonel Henry Bouquet in the north and were no longer to take orders from the governor as before. The Commons House responded by refusing to provide the extra pay that the Independents had received since 1721. Detachments were stationed in Charles Town, Fort Moore, Fort Augusta, and Fort Prince George. The uniforms at this time were probably quite similar to those described for this regiment in 1757, although various changes were gradually being effected which were confirmed by the royal warrant of 1768.

Lieutenant Governor Bull reported to the Board of Trade in November 1765 that when the tax stamps were received, he sent them to Fort Johnson for safe-keeping. He reinforced the small garrison of Provincials there with a sergeant and twelve men from the 60th Foot. Both Bull and the *Gazette* reported that no attempt was made to take the stamps from the fort. (John Drayon, in his *Memoirs of the American Revolution,* says otherwise but apparently confused the actual capture of the fort in 1775 with the civil disorders of 1765 when no attempt was made to enter the fort.)

In 1765, Fort Prince George was repaired by the soldiers of the 60th in its garrison, and work was started on a new fort, Fort Charlotte, to replace Fort Moore. The new fort was located on the Savannah River near the Long Canes settlement and was being constructed of stone from a nearby quarry. It was completed the following year and garrisoned by the detachment from Fort Moore.

General Gage in June 1768 ordered the three companies of the 60th to return to New York. The detachment in Charles Town embarked in the schooner Hawke and sailed August 7; the detachments from Fort Augusta, Fort Charlotte, and Fort Prince George departed in H.M.S. *Fowery* on August 28. Caretakers were appointed for the two South Carolina forts which were no longer garrisoned.

In 1768 the number of British troops in East Florida had grown too large for the facilities at St. Augustine. To relieve the congestion, a company of Royal Artillery and a batallion of the Royal Scots Fusiliers (21st Regiment of Foot) were sent to Charles Town for quartering in the barracks built there in 1758.

The first two companies of the 21st Foot arrived on December 29 and the other companies continued coming in small sloops and schooners through the first week in March 1769 when the full battalion was accounted for. Late in March a company of the Royal Regiment of Artillery, commanded by Captain Gostling, arrived and was quartered in the barracks.

The Artillery Company sailed for St. Augustine in August and the 21st Foot early in September. However, because of weather the three transports carrying the 21st were unable to enter St. Augustine and were blown out to sea. By October 18, all three had come back to Charles Town and the regiment was transferred to several small sloops and schooners which could use the inland waterways to St. Augustine. The 21st sailed on November 4 and finally reached its destination but only after one of the schooners grounded and sank off the entrance at St. Augustine with no loss of life. They were the last British troops to serve in South Carolina until the landing on the Isle of Palms in June 1776.

The 21st, being a Royal regiment, wore a uniform with

dark blue facings like that of the Royal Scots (1st Foot)
but its battalion companies wore fusilier caps which were
similar to the grenadier cap but not quite as tall. However, the Clothing Warrant of 1768 replaced the grenadier
caps with black bearskin caps of a similar shape. (It is not
known whether the 21st was wearing the old cloth or the
new fur fusilier cap at this date.) The warrant also specified white waistcoats, breeches, and coat linings for the
21st. The officers now wore gold lace on the coats but not
on waistcoats, with gold epaulettes (two for the grenadiers
and light infantry but only one for the battalion companies) instead of the aiguillette. Sergeants and privates
wore white lace on the coats and white metal buttons with
the regimental number on them. The white (dress) gaiters
were replaced with black.

The uniform of the Royal Regiment of Artillery was
much the same as before except for a change to white
waistcoats and breeches, the former being without lace.
Officers continued to wear aiguillettes until about 1770
before changing to epaulettes.

Selected Bibliography

Alden, John R., *John Stuart and the Southern Colonial Frontier*. Ann Arbor, 1944.

Crane, Verner W., *The Southern Frontier*. Ann Arbor, 1929.

Lawson, Cecil C. P., *The History of the Uniforms of the British Army*, Vols. II, III, IV. London, 1941, 1961, 1966.

McCrady, Edward, *The History of South Carolina*, Vols. I, II. New York, 1899, 1901.

Meriwether, Robert L., *The Expansion of South Carolina*. Kingsport, Tennessee, 1940.

Salley, Alexander S., Jr., Editor, *Narratives of Early Carolina*. New York, 1911.

Sirmans, M. Eugene, *Colonial South Carolina*. Chapel Hill, 1966.

Smith, W. Roy, *South Carolina as a Royal Province*. New York, 1903.

A rough draft of this booklet, with footnotes, is available at the South Caroliniana Library, University of South Carolina.

Appendix A

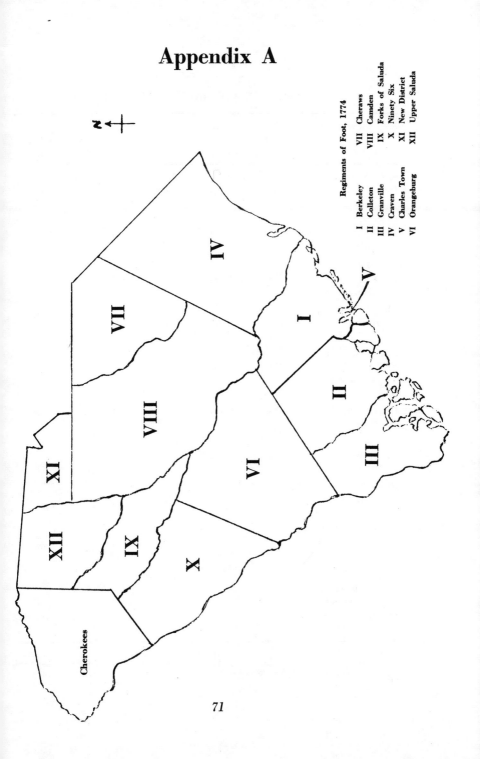

Regiments of Foot, 1774

I	Berkeley	VII	Cheraws
II	Colleton	VIII	Camden
III	Granville	IX	Forks of Saluda
IV	Craven	X	Ninety Six
V	Charles Town	XI	New District
VI	Orangeburg	XII	Upper Saluda

Cherokees

Appendix B

COLORS IN COLONIAL UNIFORMS[1]

Regiment or Company	Hat	Cockade and Feathers	Lace (on hat)	Coat	Cuffs and Coat-Lining
S. C. Reg't. of Horse, 1740 (Trooper)	black	black	silver	mazarine blue	scarlet
S. C. Reg't. of Horse, 1756 (Trooper)	black	black	gold	blue	buff
S. C. Provincial Reg't., 1757 (Private)	black	black	white	blue	buff
Charles Town Artillery Co., 1758 (Matross)	black	black	gold	blue	crimson
S. C. Provincial Reg't., 1760 (Volunteer)	black	black	silver crescent	dark green	scarlet
S. C. Provincial Reg't., 1760 (Officer)	black	black	silver crescent	blue	scarlet
S. C. Independent Co., 1760 (Officer)	black	black	silver	scarlet	light green
Royal Scots (1st Reg't. of Foot), 1760 (Grenadier)	—[2]	white tassel	white	red	dark blue
Montgomery's Highlanders (77th Reg't. of Foot), 1760 (Private)	blue	black	—	red	dark green
Royal Americans (60th Reg't. of Foot), 1764 (Sergeant)	black	black	white	scarlet	dark blue

[1] Aiguillettes and gorgets were silver; sashes were crimson.
[2] The upper front and lower back parts of the grenadier hat were dark blue; the upper back and lower front were red, as is the crown on the front. The horse and lace (piping) were white. The *GR* was gold.

72

Lapels	Buttons and Buckles	Lace	Waistcoat	Breeches	Stockings or Leggins	Belt and Cross Belts
—	silver	—	scarlet	scarlet	brown	buff
buff	brass	—	buff	blue	brown	buff
—	pewter	—	buff	blue	white	buff
crimson	brass	—	crimson	blue	white	buff
scarlet	silver	—	dark green	dark green	brown	buff
scarlet	silver	silver	blue	blue	brown	black
light green	silver	silver	scarlet	scarlet	white	buff
dark blue	pewter	white	red	blue	brown	buff
dark green	pewter	white	red	—[3]	red and white check	black
dark blue	pewter	white	scarlet	blue	brown	buff

[3]The kilt and plaid are thought to have been the military tartan which is still worn by the Black Watch (42nd Regt.), i.e., dark green, blue, and black.